A
WAY OF THE CROSS
for Children

H. J. Richards

McCRIMMONS
Great Wakering Essex

First published in Great Britain in 1986 by
McCRIMMON PUBLISHING CO LTD
Great Wakering Essex England

© 1986 Hubert Richards

ISBN 0 85597 384 6

ACKNOWLEDGEMENTS

The *Gospel texts* used here are in some cases adapted from *New World* by Alan T Dale (Oxford 1967). Grateful acknowledgement is here made for permission to make this adaptation.

The songs are taken from *Celebration Hymnal*, published by McCrimmon Publishing Co Ltd © 1976, 1981.

The photo credits are as follows:
Page 4   UNRWA photo by F Audeh
Page 6 and cover   UNRWA photo by Jack Madvo
Page 8   UNRWA photo
Page 10 Syndication International
Page 12 Syndication International
Page 14 UNWRA photo
Page 16 Photo by R J Drake
Page 18 UNRWA photo by Munir Nasr
Page 20 Photo by Mary Anne Felton
Page 22 Syndication International

Cover design Nick Snode Graphics
Printed by Mayhew McCrimmon Printers Ltd
Great Wakering Essex England

INTRODUCTION

For many hundreds of years, the friends of Jesus have held a service called the *Way of the Cross.* Some have been able to do this in Jerusalem itself, where Jesus first carried the cross. Others, who were not able to get to Jerusalem, have done it in their churches, or in their homes.

They have imagined themselves following Jesus on his last journey to his death, and stopping at various places on the way to think about him.

This book has imagined ten such places. At each one there is a short Gospel story to be read, a short thought to think about, and a short song to sing.

1.
JESUS IN AGONY

On the night before he died, Jesus took his friends into a garden to pray.
He went off a little way by himself.
He knelt down on the ground.
'Father,' he prayed, 'take this suffering away from me. Yet I will do what you want, not what I want.'
God gave him the strength he needed.
He was in very great distress, and prayed with all his heart.
So much sweat poured off him, it was as if he was bleeding. *(Luke 22: 39–44)*

Agony and pain come to all of us.
Jesus asked God to help him bear it bravely.
He wants his friends to do the same, and to pray as he did:
'I will do what you want, God, not what I want.'

Some-one's cry-ing, Lord, kum ba yah, some-one's cry-ing, Lord, kum ba yah! Some-one's cry-ing, Lord, kum ba yah! O Lord, kum ba yah.

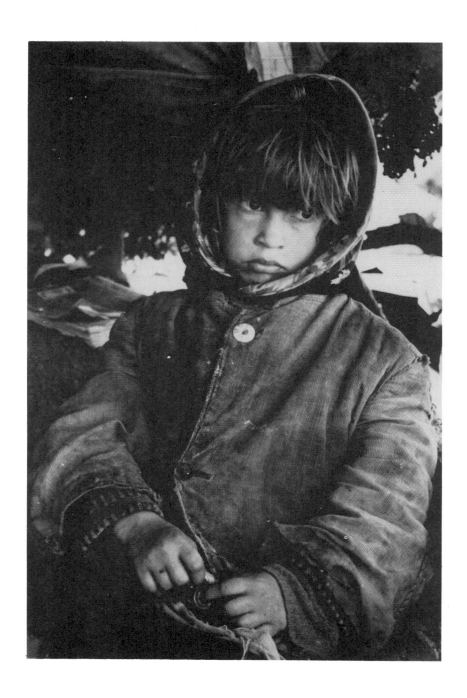

2.
JESUS ON HIS OWN

As Jesus was praying in the garden, his friend Judas came with a gang, armed with swords.
He went straight up to Jesus.
'Sir', Judas said, and kissed him.
The men grabbed Jesus, and put him under guard.
Everybody left him and ran away.
(Mark 14: 43–50)

When it came to the crunch, Jesus was left on his own.
All his friends let him down.
Judas, a very close friend, turned against him.
Peter, whom Jesus had chosen as leader, pretended he didn't know him.
The rest ran away, and Jesus was on his own.

Lord, we've all suffered from loneliness.
We're glad you know what it's like.

3.
THE CROWN OF THORNS

Jesus was taken to the Roman Governor, Pilate.
Pilate had him flogged, and then turned him over to the soldiers to make fun of him.
They made a crown out of some thorn twigs, and pressed it on his head.
Then they kept saluting him with the words,
'Long live your Majesty' and slapped him on the face.

(John 19: 1–3)

Which is worse – people pushing sharp spikes into you, or people making fun of you?
Jesus had both.
Because we know this, we pray that we may find it a bit easier when the same pain comes to us.

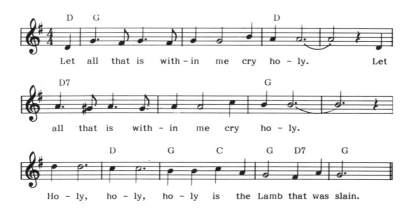

4.
JESUS TAKES UP HIS CROSS

When the soldiers had finished making fun of Jesus, they led him out to die.
They marched him off, and made him carry his own cross on his shoulders.

(John 19: 17)

Crosses come in different shapes.
Each one of us will have some cross to carry, whether we like it or not.
Jesus said the way you could tell who were his friends was the way they took up their cross.

5.
SIMON HELPS JESUS

As Jesus went on his way to die, the soldiers made a passer-by help him with his cross.
His name was Simon.
His home was in North Africa.

(Mark 15: 21)

Simon helped Jesus carry his cross.
Thank God for all the people who have helped us carry ours.
Are there some people who need me to help them carry theirs?

When I need-ed a neighbour were you there were you there? When I

need-ed a neighbour were you there? And the creed and the colour and the

name won't mat-ter were you there?

Words and Music: Sydney Carter
© Stainer & Bell Ltd.

6.
THE WOMEN COMFORT JESUS

On his way to Calvary, a large number of people followed Jesus.
Among them were a group of women, who cried for him and tried to comfort him.
Jesus told them, 'Don't cry for me. Cry for yourselves and your children.'

(Luke 22: 27–28)

Many people felt sorry for Jesus when they saw him on the way of the cross.
His mother.
The woman who wiped his face.
The women who cried for him.
Jesus felt sorry for them.
The trouble with us, Lord, is that so often we feel sorry only for ourselves.
Forgive us.

When I needed a neighbour were you there were you there? When I needed a neighbour were you there? And the creed and the colour and the name won't matter were you there?

Sydney Carter
© Stainer & Bell Ltd.

7.
JESUS ON THE CROSS

When Jesus reached Calvary, the soldiers took his clothes off him and nailed him to the cross he'd carried.
Then they tossed up for his clothes, to share them out among themselves.
(Mark 15: 22–25)

When people die, one of the saddest sights is to see the clothes they used to wear, which they'll never wear again.
It's worse when other people wear them.
Worse still if they've stolen them.
When Jesus dies, who's going to step into his shoes?

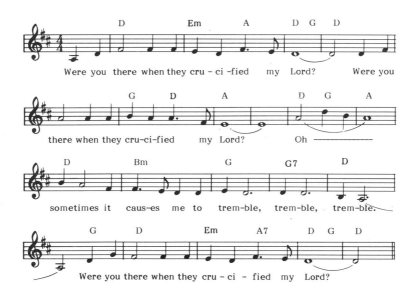

17

8.
JESUS DIES

As Jesus hung on his cross, he kept on praying:
'Father forgive them. They don't know what they're doing.'
And he prayed the words of an old hymn:
'Father, I put my whole life in your hands.'
With these words he died.
(Luke 23:34–46)

Death comes to all of us, and to all those close to us.
No one can avoid it.
It depends then how you react, whether you blame
anyone – the world we live in, other people, God.
Jesus blamed no one.
He was like God, always forgiving.

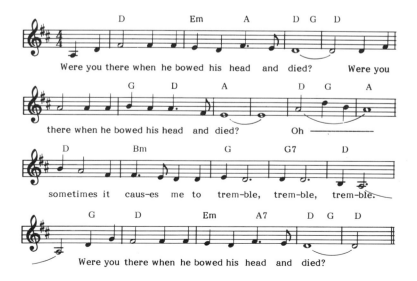

9.
JESUS IS BURIED

The friends of Jesus took his body down from the cross, and wrapped it in a linen sheet.
They put the body in a cave which had already been cut out of the rock, and rolled a stone across the front to close it.

(Mark 15: 46)

When someone has died, he is dead.
No more life.
When you bury him, you say, That's it.
It's like bricking up the doors of an empty house.
That's the end.
But burying is what you do to seeds.
Is that the end of them?

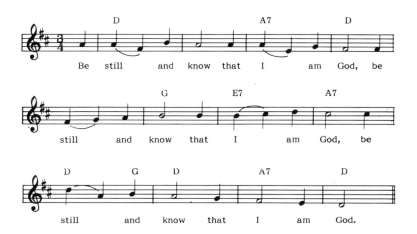

Be still and know that I am God, be
still and know that I am God, be
still and know that I am God.

10.
JESUS IS RAISED FROM THE DEAD

Very early on the Sunday morning, three women friends of Jesus came to his grave.
They found the stone had been rolled away.
They went into the cave, and were amazed to see an angel sitting there. He said:
'Don't be frightened.
You are looking for Jesus.
You won't find him here.
He has been raised from the dead.
He is alive.' *(Mark 16: 1–6)*

If you leave seeds in a packet, they remain just what they are – seeds.
If you bury them in the ground, they turn into grain and grass and flowers.
Jesus said his death would be like planting a seed.
Today the life of Jesus is everywhere.

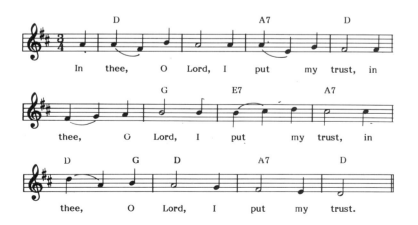

A NOTE TO MINISTERS AND TEACHERS

This service has been used successfully on Good Friday as a children's alternative to the liturgy of the day. Middle school boys and girls were chosen to read out the Gospel texts and to hold up the illustrations in large poster form. A teacher or minister read out the meditations without further comment, and a guitar was used to lead the singing. At the end, each child was given a spring flower to take home as a reminder of the meaning of Jesus' death.